WHAT WE GET FROM NORSE MYTHOLOGY

KATHERINE KRIEG

13 5-28
BOT 2850/2209

Published in the United States of America
by Cherry Lake Publishing
Ann Arbor, Michigan
www.cherrylakepublishing.com

Consultants: Lars Jenner, Lecturer, Department of Scandinavian Studies, University of Washington; Marla Conn, ReadAbility, Inc.
Editorial direction and book production: Red Line Editorial

Photo Credits: Dreamstime, cover, 1; William Rossin/Hemera/Thinkstock, 5; Shutterstock Images, 7; Dorling Kindersley/Thinkstock, 8; Michael Nicholson/Corbis, 11; Bettmann/Corbis, 12; Árni Magnússon Institute, 14; Christel Gerstenberg/Corbis, 17; Mårten Eskil Winge, 18; Werner Forman/Corbis, 21; Lilli Strauss/AP Images, 23; Marvel Entertainment/AP Images, 25; Jay Maidment/Walt Disney Studios/Everett Collection, 26; Walt Disney Pictures/Everett Collection, 28

Library of Congress Cataloging-in-Publication Data

Krieg, Katherine, author.
  What we get from Norse mythology / by Katherine Krieg.
    pages cm. -- (Mythology and culture)
  Includes index.
  ISBN 978-1-63188-914-1 (hardcover : alk. paper) -- ISBN 978-1-63188-930-1 (pbk. : alk. paper) -- ISBN 978-1-63188-946-2 (pdf) -- ISBN 978-1-63188-962-2 (hosted ebook)
  1. Mythology, Norse--Juvenile literature. 2. Civilization, Viking--Influence--Juvenile literature. I. Title.

  BL860.K75 2015
  398.2'0948--dc23

                    2014029991

Cherry Lake Publishing would like to acknowledge the work of
The Partnership for 21st Century Skills. Please visit *www.p21.org*
for more information.

Printed in the United States of America
Corporate Graphics
December 2014

ABOUT THE AUTHOR

Katherine Krieg is the author of many books for young people. She enjoys learning about the different gods and goddesses in Norse mythology.

TABLE OF CONTENTS

CHAPTER 1

AMAZING STORIES

A warrior god slays giants with one strike of his mighty hammer. A goddess weeps golden tears. An eight-legged magical horse rides across a rainbow bridge. All of these things happen in Norse **mythology**.

Mythologies are collections of legendary stories. Throughout history, many cultures have developed mythologies to explain the world around them. The invented characters and stories of mythologies reflect a culture's ideas and values.

Norse **myths** originated centuries ago. The stories changed over time as different people retold them. The myths reveal how the Norse people viewed the world around them and what they valued most. Similarly, the ways these myths are retold today can reveal what is

An eight-legged horse named Sleipnir is one of the many amazing creatures from Norse mythology.

important in our **modern** culture. Like other major mythologies in history, Norse mythology features themes and characters that are still relevant today.

Norse myths came from an area in Europe called Scandinavia. This area includes the places that are now the countries of Norway, Sweden, Denmark, and Iceland. The earliest record of the Norse people appears near the end of the 700s CE.

Historians believe Norse myths were more than just stories for Norse people. For some, the mythology was a religion. These people believed in the gods from the stories they told. One popular god, Thor, carried a powerful hammer as a weapon.

Around the year 800, people living in Scandinavia came into contact with people living in the British Isles. In writings from the time, the people of the British Isles called the Scandinavians who arrived on ships Vikings. These Vikings attacked **monasteries** on the British coast. They stole gold, books, and other resources from

ICELAND

NORWAY

SWEDEN

BRITISH ISLES

NORTH
SEA

DENMARK

ATLANTIC
OCEAN

LOOK AGAIN

ANCIENT NORSE PEOPLE LIVED IN THESE AREAS.
WHY MIGHT THE VIKINGS HAVE TARGETED
THE BRITISH ISLES WITH THEIR RAIDS?

Viking warriors traveled in boats known as longships.

the monasteries. Monasteries were easy targets for the Vikings because the buildings were not defended.

The Vikings learned about Christianity from the people on the British Isles. Christianity was already common among the people living there. Some Vikings began practicing Christianity too. Many of them continued to worship their original gods at the same time.

The Norse myths that we know about today were written down by Christian **priests** around 1250. These priests saw the Norse stories as **folklore** or myths, not as a valid religion. Most of the myths were written down as poetry. But the priests probably weren't the first people to write down the myths. They likely copied other manuscripts that have since been lost. Snorri Sturluson, an Icelandic poet, wrote two books of Norse mythology, *Prose Edda* and *Heimskringla,* in the 1200s. These books account for most of what is known about Norse mythology.

CHAPTER 2

GODS AND CREATURES

Norse mythology is full of exciting figures and stories. With characters ranging from magical animals to powerful gods, it is no wonder people are still interested in these tales.

In Norse mythology, there are nine separate worlds. Different creatures live in each world. Humans live in Midgard, or "Middle Earth." A rainbow bridge connects Midgard to Asgard, the world of the gods. Through this link, Norse people believed gods could interact with the

In Norse mythology, Odin and Frigg live in a world called Asgard.

human world. The remaining worlds were home to giants, elves, and other creatures.

Several Norse myths are about Odin, the ruler of Asgard and the other gods. Odin had a wife named Frigg. One myth tells the story of how Odin and his two brothers, Vili and Vé, destroyed a frost-giant called Ymir. Then, they used Ymir's body to create the world. Ymir's eyebrows created Midgard, where humans would live. Although he was a war god, Odin also stressed the importance of logic and reason. He spoke in **verse**. Odin owned a magical eight-legged horse named Sleipnir. He could ride the horse across land, through water, and in the air.

The best-known god in Norse mythology is Odin's son Thor, the fierce god of thunder. Thor had a mighty hammer he used to kill evil giants. He sometimes wore a belt that made him even stronger. Thor rode through the sky in a chariot pulled by two goats. He could kill and eat the goats. Then he could bring them back to life with his magical hammer.

Norse mythology also features many goddesses. Freya was the goddess of love and **fertility**. She was said to ride on a boar that had golden hairs or in a chariot pulled by cats. According to one myth, when Freya's

Thor is known for his magical hammer, called Mjölnir.

husband Od went on long journeys, Freya cried tears
of gold.

Not all Norse gods were good. The god Loki often
played tricks on other gods. Loki could change into any

form. In one story, he tricks a blind god into killing another god. In some stories, Loki helps the other gods. For example, he assists Thor in retrieving his hammer

Loki was seen as a trickster god.

after giants steal it. But Loki is disloyal to the gods in most stories.

Norse mythology is filled with creatures of all kinds. Stories of giants, elves, trolls, and dwarves are common. Some creatures were good and helpful, while others caused problems for gods and humans alike. Elves, for example, were thought to be beautiful creatures that caused human illnesses but also had the ability to heal people.

GO DEEPER

DISCUSS WHAT YOU'VE LEARNED ABOUT NORSE MYTHOLOGY WITH A FRIEND. WHICH STORIES TOLD IN THIS CHAPTER ARE THE MOST SURPRISING TO YOU? WHY?

CHAPTER 3

WISDOM AND TRICKS

Although the Norse myths were first told a long time ago, they still affect the stories and culture of today. You may not have heard about characters with names such as Odin or Freya, but they have deeply influenced modern culture.

Odin was viewed as a god of poetry, discovering poetry and providing it for gods and humans. In Norse myths, Odin often speaks in verse. This type of **heroic**, intelligent figure is still seen today in fictional wizards

Odin was seen as both a warrior and a wise poet.

and real-life scientists. People continue to respect the
wise and educated.

Odin and his son Thor are similar to other muscled
heroes in modern culture. Since ancient times, there
have been stories of strong characters achieving
amazing feats. In Norse mythology, Thor grappled with
giants. We see a similar focus on physical strength today
in the world of sports. Seeing and hearing about people

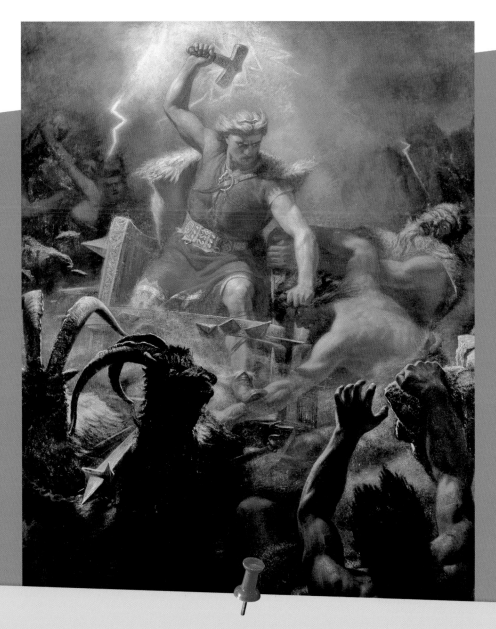

LOOK AGAIN

Look closely at this illustration of Thor in battle. Does it remind you of the feats of athletic strength that people like to watch today? What does the image tell you about how the artist views Thor?

achieving incredible feats of strength continue to be a draw for many people.

Tricksters such as Loki are another common theme in modern movies, books, and plays. In Norse mythology, Loki was said to be stunningly handsome. Think about villains in your favorite books or movies. Handsome villains still pop up in the media today. Often, as was the case with Loki, villains are able to trick others into thinking they have good intentions by charming them with their appearance or skills.

CHAPTER 4

WORDS AND ART

Have you ever accused your sister of going **berserk** when someone plays her favorite song? Have you ever made plans to meet up with your friends on a Friday? You may not realize it, but Norse mythology has an impact on your daily life through the words you speak.

More than 5,000 words in the English language come from the Old Norse language. *Berserk* is one of them. This word refers to Norse warriors who went out of control in battles and fought wildly.

Some of the names for the days of the week that we use today came from Norse mythology. Tuesday, Wednesday, Thursday, and Friday were all named for Norse gods or goddesses. Tuesday is named after Tyr, a god who usually shows up in Norse myths as Odin's son. Odin himself lent his name to Wednesday.

Tyr is featured on this Viking artifact dating to the 500s CE.

Odin was often pronounced *Wodan*. So, Wednesday was Wodan's day. Thursday was named after Thor. Friday comes from the name of Odin's wife, Frigg.

German composer Richard Wagner made use of Norse mythology in his 1870 opera *The Valkyrie*. The opera is named after the Valkyries—female figures in Norse mythology who decided which warriors would die on the battlefield and which would survive. The story of Wagner's opera features the Germanic equivalents of the gods Odin and Frigg. Wagner based the opera on Norse mythological tales, including the writings of

THINK ABOUT IT

Does it surprise you that words we use often, such as the days of the week, come from Norse mythology? Discuss what you learned in this chapter with a classmate.

Wagner's opera is still performed often today.

Snorri Sturluson. One section, known as "Ride of the Valkyries," features one of the most famous pieces of music in history.

CHAPTER 5

MYTHS IN BOOKS AND MOVIES

Parts of Norse mythology may already be familiar to you. Marvel Comics introduced Thor as a comic book hero in 1962. More recently, there have been several movies starring this version of Thor. They include *Thor* and *Thor: The Dark World*. Thor also appeared in *The Avengers*.

Other characters from Norse mythology, including Loki, Odin, and Frigg, also show up in these movies. In Marvel's telling, Loki and Thor are adopted brothers. In *Thor*, Thor tries to stop Loki from taking over Asgard.

Thor has been a major comic book character for more than 50 years.

In *The Avengers*, Loki tries to launch an alien invasion of Earth. Thor and other superheroes, including Iron Man and Captain America, stop him. These stories do not

LOOK AGAIN

Does Marvel's Thor look the same as you imagined Thor from the Norse myths?

[21ST CENTURY SKILLS LIBRARY]

have roots in Norse mythology. Only a few of the characters are shared with the real myths.

The author of the Lord of the Rings series, J. R. R. Tolkien, was interested in Norse mythology. He used parts of it in his books. For example, Tolkien likely based the wizard Gandalf's appearance on Odin. In some myths, Odin looks like an old wizard when he travels in the human world. Additionally, Tolkien borrowed many creatures from Norse mythology, such as elves, trolls, and dwarves. Tolkien also based his universe for the Lord of the Rings books after the separate worlds in Norse mythology. Most notably, Tolkien introduces a land called Middle-earth—the main area where his stories take place.

Although the popular Disney film *Frozen* was loosely based on the fairy tale "The Snow Queen," written by Hans Christian Andersen in the 1800s, it is clear that Andersen was influenced by Norse mythology. Disney based the *Frozen* character Elsa on Andersen's

The character of Elsa from Frozen *has a connection
to characters from Norse mythology.*

Snow Queen. Some people believe Andersen used the
Norse goddess Skadi as a model for the character of the
Snow Queen. A giant goddess, Skadi lived high in the
mountains and usually wore snowshoes or skis.

In many ways, Norse mythology still influences our world. From language to comic books to movies, the **legacy** of Norse characters and themes is still visible. Understanding these Norse myths can give us a better awareness of the many mythological stories common in our culture today.

THINK ABOUT IT

WHY DO YOU THINK MARVEL AND TOLKIEN BORROWED NORSE CHARACTERS AND THEMES? HOW DID THEY CHANGE THE MYTHOLOGY FOR MODERN AUDIENCES?

THINK ABOUT IT

- Find a reliable Web site about Norse mythology. What else can you learn about the stories? Is there variety in how the tales are told? What is the same? What is different?

- In Chapter One, you read about where Norse mythology developed. Research what the climate is like in this region. How might the climate have impacted the stories that the Norse people developed?

- This book discusses Norse gods that have both intelligence and physical strength. Can you think of any examples of modern characters like this?

LEARN MORE

FURTHER READING

Ganeri, Anita. *Norse Myths and Legends*. Chicago: Raintree, 2013.

Green, Roger Lancelyn. *Myths of the Norsemen*. London: Puffin Classics, 2013.

Philip, Neil. *Eyewitness Mythology*. New York: DK Publishing, 2011.

WEB SITES

How Stuff Works: The Vikings
http://history.howstuffworks.com/historical-figures/viking.htm
Read this Web site for more information about Viking myths, ships, weapons, and culture.

Vikings: Beliefs and Stories
http://www.bbc.co.uk/schools/primaryhistory/vikings/beliefs_and_stories
This Web site includes a timeline of Viking history and more information about the gods, goddesses, and creatures of Norse mythology.

GLOSSARY

berserk (ber-ZERK) wild and out of control

fertility (fur-TILL-uh-tee) the capability to create new life

folklore (FOHK-lor) stories passed down through generations within a community

heroic (hi-ROH-ik) like a hero

legacy (LEG-uh-see) something handed down from the past

modern (MOD-urn) happening recently

monasteries (MON-uh-ster-eez) places where monks or nuns live

mythology (mi-THOL-uh-jee) a collection of myths dealing with a culture's gods or heroes

myths (MITHS) stories that attempt to describe the origin of a people's customs or beliefs or to explain mysterious events

priests (PREESTS) people who lead churches or congregations

verse (VURSS) rhyming or rhythmic poetry

INDEX